Dehydrator Cookbook

The Complete Beginner's Guide to Dehydrate, Preserve and Store Food with Simple and Healthy Recipes

Michelle Vazquez

ISBN-13: 979- 8567654781

DEDICATION

To all who desire to live life to the fullest!

TABLE OF CONTENT

INTRODUCTION

Food dehydration is the removal of water and moisture from fruits, vegetables, fish and meat either through sun drying, an oven or a dehydrator to preserve these foods from microorganism and bacteria while keeping the nutrients intact.

Drying out food is an ancient practice, where individuals dry their seeds out under the sun for later use. But, considering the modern day's focus on cheap and fast food, people have gotten to comfortable and subsequently ignored the thought about the processes, additives and preservatives that go into preparing their favorite fast foods.

Why should you dehydrate your food?

There's practically no simpler method to preserve food than dehydration. Used over the years to store food without refrigeration, dehydration is the quickest and most economical method of food storage and preservation. It also comes in handy when making travel plans, outdoor camping or long duration tours.

WHAT IS A FOOD DEHYDRATOR?

A food dehydrator is a small kitchen appliance used to dehydrate and get moisture out of your food. With the aid of an in-built fan, and low temperature, the dehydrator reduces the quantity of water or moisture present in fruits, meats, fish, vegetables and all sort of food item.

Once reduced, the risk of decomposition of the food is cut down and the nutrients kept, making the food eligible for storage over a long period, assuming the moisture in the food is dried out to at least 90%.

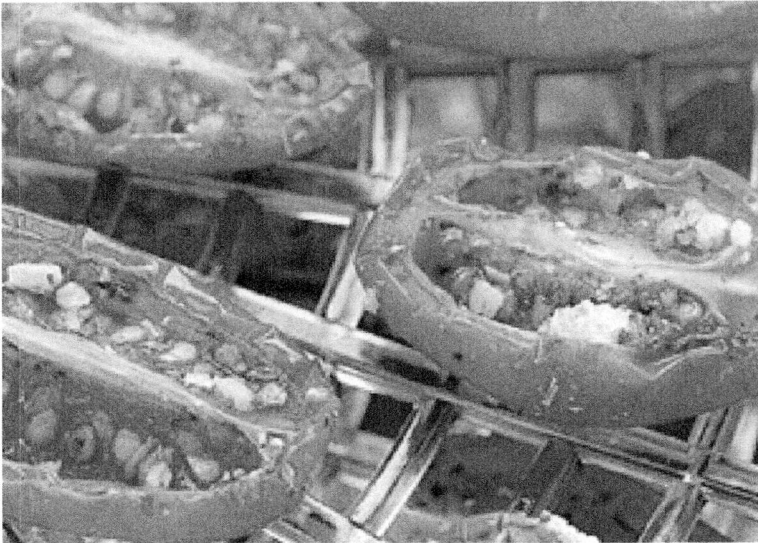

Types of Food Dehydration

There are different approaches to dry food out, however, some approaches are more effective than others and this is because of the advancement in technology which plays a major role in how well foods get dehydrated.

Below are some of the most popular methods of dehydrating food, including both the modern and traditional methods.

- **Sun Drying**

Sun drying is the oldest and cheapest method of dehydrating and preserving food. For over 11000 years, people have cut open their foods and spread it out under the sun to dry. Dehydration under the sun is mostly effective in regions that experience a prolonged time of hot sunshine or with a temperature minimum of 86°F. All these processes usually take many days however, it is very cheap and still effective.

- **Solar Drying**

Solar drying is an upgrade from the direct sun drying. It is the dehydration of food with a solar powered dehydrator. Solar dehydrator draws energy from the sun and convert that energy into hot air that dries out your food.

- **Air Drying**

Air drying is very similar to sun drying and has also been around for a very long time. The only difference between sun drying and air drying is that air drying is done under a shade that shield the food from a direct contact with the sun's rays.

I usually advise this for delicate herbs and vegetables that might get burnt from direct sun rays.

- **Electric Drying**

With modern technology came the extinction of ancient methods. Electric dehydrators are built with modern elements and fan that allow the quick and efficient dehydration of your food. This ensures no damage to the food and a healthy and tasty dehydrated food.

An electric dehydrator allows you to speed up or reduce the dehydration rate of your food, and it remains the best method to dehydration.

- **Excalibur Drying**

Drying with an Excalibur is best suited for natural products like fruits, fruit leathers, vegetables, herbs, jerky, fish, grains and nuts.

- **Oven Drying**

This is the use of an oven to slowly dehydrate your food at a temperature of 140°F or else the food will get cooked. Because of how small ovens are, they are not the best option for dehydrating large quantity of food and will require that you dehydrate in small batches.

But for small and quick dehydration, oven drying is a great option.

Tips to an Effective Dehydration

Here are some fundamental tips to an effective food dehydration that you should keep at the back of your mind.

- **Proper Preparation**

Before dehydrating any food item, ensure to thoroughly wash the items with clean running water and dry them out before transferring into the dehydrator. Make use of a glove when handling food items you want to dehydrate. Chop the food item into even sizes.

- **Ensure you have the correct temperature degrees**

The temperature and time needed to sufficiently get your food dried out will change contingent upon the type of dehydrator you are using and the food you are dehydrating. This cookbook includes recommended dehydration time and temperature levels for each recipe.

- **Be Patient**

Proper dehydration takes time, so it's best not to be in a hurry. Don't increase the dehydrator temperature in order to reduce the dehydration time, as this might eventually burn out or cook the food. Take your time and allow the food to get dry at its own pace.

- **Ensure up to 90% dehydration**

In order to guarantee expected dehydration results, it is best to allow the food to get dehydrated up to a minimum of 90%. When the food item still feels sticky, soft or light, it is best to return it into the dehydrator and dry it out for some extra minutes.

Food items that can be dehydrated

Grains; buckwheat, rice, quinoa, barley, amaranth

Herbs; basil, oregano, dill, parsley, mint, fennel, hyssop

Seeds & nuts; hazelnuts, walnuts, pecans, almonds, macadamia

Vegetables; mushrooms, carrots, peas, onions, tomatoes, beans

Fruits; bananas, apples, peaches, apricots, cherries, pears, blueberries

Meat & fish; chicken, ground beef, turkey, cured meats, sliced meats, beef jerky, fresh fish

HOW TO STORE DEHYDRATED FOODS

The level of dryness of any food item totally depends on your individual preference, but for proper preservation of food, before storing, you have to first ensure the food is completely dry and with no moisture or water in them. At least you should strive for 90% dryness, ensuring only 10% of moisture left in the food item.

To check the dryness of the food item, you can press the food between your thumbs or cut it open to make sure it is no longer sticky and left with no moisture, then set aside and allow it to cool off.

Using a clean, dry and an airtight container, store in the dehydrated food and keep in a place cool and out of direct sunlight rays. Storage duration for food item varies, but most can stay up to 12 months when properly dehydrated.

Benefits of Dehydrating

There are many benefits associated with dehydrating your food. From saving your time and money to providing you with an optimal health, in this chapter you will get to understand why food dehydration is good for you and your family.

Below are six benefits of dehydrating your food.

- **Naturally Nutritious**

Food items are dehydrated in their raw forms, which leaves them a 100% natural, allowing you to benefit from all the nutrients present in the food such as; iron, magnesium carotene & vitamin C that would have been lost if cooked due to high exposure to heat or processed with chemicals and additives.

- **No Preservatives or Chemicals**

When dehydrating raw foods, there are no needs to add any preservative, additive, trans sugar or chemicals. By preparing your own dehydrated foods, you provide yourself and your family with healthy chemical-free foods that are not loaded with chemicals like sulfur dioxide or refined sugar, which are hazardous to your health.

- **Reduces waste & saves your money**

With the frequent hike in food prices, the cheapness of buying in bulk, dehydrating your food will help you save the extra cents you would have used to buy during a hike in price. Dehydration also helps to curtail wastage, as you could easily dehydrate excess leftovers than having to discard them due to their short shelf lives.

- **Easy Storage and Preservation**

Dehydration helps to preserve the shelf life of various food items far longer than it should be, and the reduction of moisture from these items makes it easier to store than regular food items.

- **Low Risk of Bacteria and Contamination**

When properly dehydrated and stored, dehydrated foods have a lower risk of been contaminated, making sure your food items stay healthy throughout its storage life.

- **Portable**

Dehydrating food shrinks down the sizes of food items by removing the moisture present in the food. This makes it easier for the food items to be carried about and around in case of emergency and need for a quick food pack.

VEGGIES

Dehydrated Applesauce & Potato Leather

Preparation Time: 7 minutes

Dehydration Time: 3-5 hours

Ingredients

1/4 cup raw honey

1 teaspoon cinnamon

2 cups unsweetened applesauce

2 cups sweet potatoes, cooked & mashed

sea salt, to taste

13

Instructions

1. Using a high speed blender, add in all the ingredients and blend until smooth, adding water is needed.

2. Transfer the mixture onto a dehydrator sheet, spread around into thin and even thickness.

3. Dehydrate until leathery at 100°F with no moisture left.

4. Serve and enjoy or store in a dry place until ready to devour.

Simple Pumpkin Dehydrator Leather

Preparation Time: 15 minutes

Dehydration Time: 12 hours

Ingredients

1/4 cup honey

1/4 cup shredded coconut

1/2 teaspoon ground nutmeg

1/2 teaspoon ground allspice

1 cup coconut milk

1 teaspoon ground cinnamon

2 cups pumpkin

2 cups unsweetened applesauce

2 tablespoons chopped raisins

Instructions

1. Using a large mixing bowl, combine all the ingredients together until mixed and incorporated.

2. Transfer the mixture onto a dehydrator sheet then transfer into a dehydrator and dehydrate for 12 hours at 135°F.

3. Cut the leathers into a desired shape, roll up, serve and enjoy or store for later use.

Dehydrating Jalapeño Peppers

Preparation Time: 15 minutes

Dehydration Time: 8-12 hours

Ingredients

jalapeno peppers

Instructions

1. Wash the peppers and dry then stem and vertically halve them.

2. Take the seeds out of the peppers and pit then transfer onto a dehydrator tray.

3. Dehydrate for 8-12 hours at 140°F.

4. Once dehydrated, store in an airtight container until ready to use.

Orange, Sauce & Yogurt Leather

Preparation Time: 10 minutes

Dehydration Time: 7 hours

Ingredients

1 cup applesauce

1 orange juice can

32 ounces vanilla yogurt

Instructions

1. Using a high speed blender, process all the ingredients until smooth and combined.

2. Transfer the mixture onto the dehydrator sheet and spread out into a thin and even level.

3. Dehydrate the mix until leather for 7 hours at 135°F.

4. Serve and enjoy or store for later use.

Cauliflower Popcorn

Preparation Time: 10 minutes

Dehydration Time: 10 hours

Ingredients

1/2 teaspoon ground cumin

1 cauliflower head

1 tablespoon paprika

1 teaspoon smoked cayenne

3 tablespoons olive oil

4 tablespoons hot sauce

Instructions

1. Wash the cauliflower, dry then chop into florets and coat with a mixture of the remaining ingredients.

2. Transfer the coated florets onto a dehydrator tray then dehydrate until dried at 130°F for 10 hours.

3. Serve and enjoy or store in a cool dry place for later.

Simple Zucchini Fruit Chips

Preparation Time: 10 minutes

Dehydration Time: 15 hours

Ingredients

1 cup water

1 can grape juice

8 cups zucchini

Instructions

1. Deseed the zucchini then boil all the ingredients together and simmer for 30 minutes until the vegetable is translucent.

2. Drain the zucchini and allow to cool off then bake in the oven on a parchment paper for 15 hours at 135°F until dried.

3. Serve immediately and enjoy or refrigerate for up to a week.

Dehydrating Beet Chips

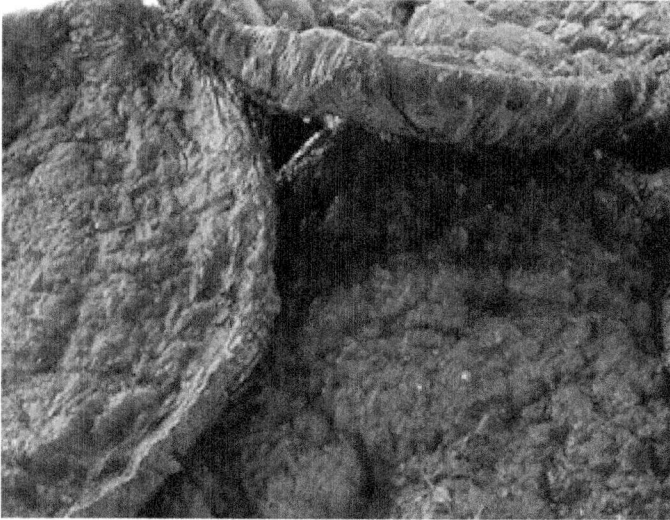

Preparation Time: 15 minutes

Dehydration Time: 10-12 hours

Ingredients

1/4 teaspoon sea salt

1/4 teaspoon powdered onion

1/4 teaspoon powdered garlic

1 tablespoon coconut oil

red organic large beets

Instructions

1. Rinse and dry the beets then chop off the tops.

2. Chop the beets into 1/4" size bits then coat with the spices, salt and oil until well covered.

3. Arrange the chopped beets on the dehydrator tray then dehydrate for 10-12 hours at 140°F.

4. Once done, store in an airtight container until ready to use.

Simple Baked Cucumber Snacks

Preparation Time: 10 minutes

Dehydration Time: 11 hours

Ingredients

1 tablespoon vegetable oil

2 medium cucumbers

2 teaspoons apple cider vinegar

sea salt, to taste

Instructions

1. Chop the cucumber into tiny pieces then squeeze out excess moisture and coat with the remaining ingredients.

2. Arrange the coated pieces on a dehydrator tray and dehydrate for 11 hours at 130°F until crispy.

3. Serve and enjoy or store for later.

Dehydrating Green Beans

Preparation Time: 7 minutes

Dehydration Time: 6-8 hours

Ingredients

fresh green beans

Instructions

1. Wash the green beans and dry then cut off the ends and blanch for 3 minutes in a boiling water.

2. Arrange the blanched green beans on the dehydrator tray then dehydrate for 6-8 hours at 130°F.

3. Once dry, store in an airtight container in a cool and dry place.

Simple Bell Pepper Dehydration

Preparation Time: 10 minutes

Dehydration Time: 12-24 hours

Ingredients

bell pepper of choice

Instructions

1. Chop the bell peppers into small pieces then remove the seed.

2. Arrange the chopped pepper on the dehydrator tray then place inside the dehydrator.

3. Dehydrate the peppers for 12-24 hours at 125°F until completely dried.

4. Store in a cool and dry place until ready to use.

Pickles Chips

Preparation Time: 0 minute

Dehydration Time: 4-6 hours

Ingredients

1 jar of pickles

Instructions

1. Arrange the pickles on a dehydrator tray then dehydrate for 4-6 hours at 135°F.

2. Serve and enjoy or store for later use.

Dehydrated Okra Pods

Preparation Time: 15 minutes

Dehydration Time: 24 hours

Ingredients

15 pods okra

Instructions

1. Rinse and dry the okra pods then chop into small rings fit for frying.

2. Arrange the okra pods in a single layer on a dehydrator sheet.

3. Dehydrate for 24 hours on low setting until crispy.

4. Serve immediately and enjoy or freeze for 2 days before storing.

5. Store in a cool and dry place for later use.

Homemade Dehydrated Scallions

Preparation Time: 10 minutes

Dehydration Time: 3-5 hours

Ingredients

green onions

Instructions

1. Slice the root ends of the onions off then wash and dry.

2. Chop the scallions into small even sizes then separate the white rings.

3. Arrange the scallions on a dehydrator tray then dehydrate at 95°F for 3-5 hours until done.

4. Use and enjoy or store for later.

Dehydrated Celery Bits

Preparation Time: 10 minutes

Dehydration Time: 8-15 hours

Ingredients

chopped celery

Instructions

1. Rinse and dry the chopped celery then arrange on a dehydrator tray.

2. Dehydrate the celery for 8-15 hours at 125°F-135°F.

3. Use and enjoy or store for later.

Tomato & Walnuts Dehydrated Crackers

Preparation Time: 20 minutes

Dehydration Time: 13 hours

Ingredients

1/4 cup water

1/4 cup diced olives

1/3 cup chopped sun-dried tomatoes

1/2 cup ground flax

1 teaspoon oregano

2 cups soaked walnuts

salt & thyme, to taste

Instructions

1. Using a high speed blender, add in the soaked walnuts and process until powdered.

2. Add in the flax meal and incorporate then remove from the blender and set aside.

3. Add the tomatoes, olives and water into the blender and process together.

4. Incorporate the tomatoes mixture and flax meal together then add in the spices and combine.

5. Transfer the dough out onto a dehydrator sheet and spread out into 1/4" thickness.

6. Dehydrate for 1 hour at 140°F then 115°F for 12 hours until dry, flipping the crackers halfway through Dehydration Time.

7. Serve and enjoy or store for later use.

Dehydrating Frozen Veggies

Preparation Time: 0 minute

Dehydration Time: 6-8 hours

Ingredients

a pack of frozen veggies

Instructions

1. Arrange the frozen vegetables on the dehydrator tray.

2. Dehydrate for 6-8 hours at 125°F.

3. Store in an airtight container until ready to use.

Cheesy Garlic Zucchini Chips

Preparation Time: 13 minutes

Dehydration Time: 5-10 hours

Ingredients

1/8 teaspoon salt

1 minced garlic clove

1 pound sliced thin zucchini

1 ounce grated Parmesan cheese

1 teaspoon apple cider vinegar

Instructions

1. Place the chopped zucchini in a medium sized bowl then add in the garlic, cheese, salt, vinegar and combine together.

2. Arrange the coated zucchini slices on the dehydrator tray then dehydrate until crispy for 5-10 hours at 135°F.

3. Store in an air tight container until ready to use.

Dehydrating Onions into Flakes & Powder

Preparation Time: 15 minutes

Dehydration Time: 3-9 hours

Ingredients

onions

Instructions

1. Remove the skins of the onions then cut off the ends and dice into even sized pieces.

2. Separate the onion segments then arrange in a single layer on the dehydrator tray.

3. Dehydrate for 3-9 hours at 125°F until crisp and dry.

4. Allow the onion pieces to cool off then crush into flakes or powder if desired.

5. Store using an airtight container until ready to use.

Simple Rolled Oats Dehydration

Preparation Time: 5 minutes

Dehydration Time: 12 hours

Ingredients

rolled oats

clean water

juiced lime

Instructions

1. Using a large mixing bowl, pour in the rolled oats, a cup of water and combine together until mixed.

2. Pour in the juiced lime and combine together until mixed then set aside to sit for 24 hours.

3. Like a large dehydrator tray, spread the oats out in a thin layer on the baking sheet.

4. Setting the temperature to 135°F, dehydrate until dry for 12 hours.

5. Once dehydrated, store in a cool and dry place until ready to use.

Dehydrating Marinated Eggplant Slices

Preparation Time: 20 minutes

Dehydration Time: 12-16 hours

Ingredients

1/4 cup vinegar

1/4 cup avocado oil

1/4 cup maple syrup

1/4 cup low salt tamari

1 teaspoon smoked paprika

1 1/2 pounds rinsed & stemmed eggplant, rinsed, stem removed, and sliced to 1/4-inch in long strips

2 teaspoons chili powder

salt & cayenne pepper, to taste

Instructions

1. Vertically slice the eggplants into 1/2" long strips then arrange on a large baking dish and set aside.

2. Using a small mix bowl, add in all the marinade ingredients and combine together.

3. Pour the marinade mix into the baking dish then toss the eggplant slices over until well coated then set aside to marinate for an hour.

4. Arrange the marinated slices on a dehydrator tray then dehydrate for 12-16 hours at 140°F until the slices are crisp.

5. Once dehydrated, store in an airtight container until ready to use.

Butternut Squash Chips

Preparation Time: 15 minutes

Dehydration Time: 10-12 hours

Ingredients

1/8 teaspoon sea salt

1/4 cup pumpkin seeds

1/2 teaspoon nutmeg

1 juiced orange

1 cup of raisins

1 teaspoon ground cinnamon

4 tablespoons of maple syrup

4 cups of peeled & chopped butternut squash

cardamom to taste

Instructions

1. Using a high speed blender, add in the butternut squash and process until blended then transfer into a mixing bowl.

2. Pour in the juiced orange, raisins and blend together then pour into the blended squash mix.

3. Add the cinnamon, sweetener, salt, nutmeg, pumpkin seeds and cardamom into the squash mix and combine together, adjusting the taste as desired.

4. Prepare the dehydrator tray then scoop the squash mixture into ball and arrange on the dehydrator tray and flatten each one into 1/2" thickness.

5. Dehydrate for 10-12 hours at 105°F until dry.

6. Store in an airtight container until ready to use.

Dehydrating Potato Chunks

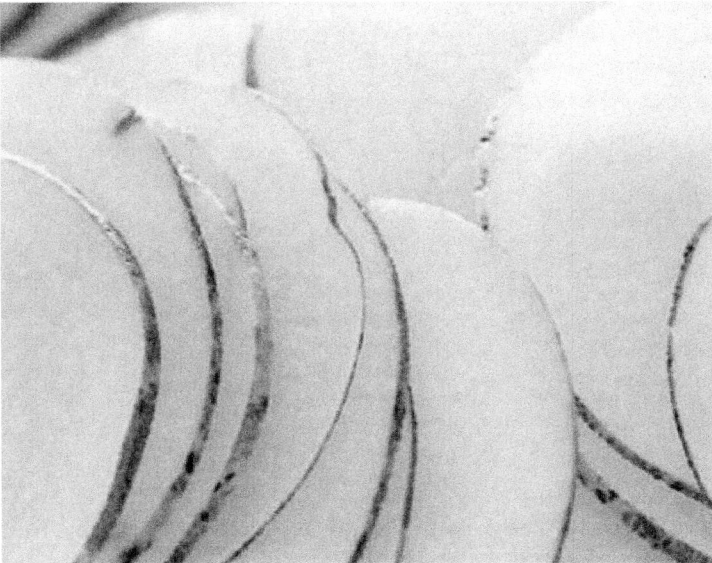

Preparation Time: 15 minutes

Dehydration Time: 6 hours

Ingredients

5 peeled & chopped potatoes

cold water

Instructions

1. Cover the potatoes with enough water then boil until tenderized for 10-15 minutes over medium heat.

2. Drain the potatoes then smash until smooth then arrange on a dehydrator tray.

3. Dehydrate until dry for 6 hours at 145°F.

4. Break the potatoes sheets into small chunks then blend into flakes and store in an air tight container in a cool and dry place.

Pepperoni Chips Dehydration

Preparation Time: 2 minutes

Dehydration Time: 1 minute

Ingredients

1 pack regular pepperonis

Instructions

1. Arrange the pepperonis in between two paper towels.

2. Transfer the paper towels with pepperonis into a microwave and heat for a minute until crispy and stiff.

3. Repeat the same process for any remaining pepperonis then store in a cool and dry place until ready to use.

Dehydrated Carrot & Parsnip Chips

Preparation Time: 10 minutes

Dehydration Time: 8-10 hours

Ingredients

1 lime juice

4 big carrots

4 big parsnips

chopped dill, as desired

salt & black pepper, to taste

Instructions

1. Rinse then peel the carrots and parsnips then chop into thin rounds.

2. Transfer the chopped veggies into a mixing bowl the pour in the lime juice, pepper, salt, dill and combine together.

3. Arrange the mixture on a dehydrator tray, then dehydrate for 8-10 hours at 114°F.

4. Store in a cool and dry place until ready to use.

FRUIT RECIPES

Simple Dehydrated Fruit Powder

Preparation Time: 10 minutes

Dehydration Time: 5-10 hours

Ingredients

any dehydrated unsweetened fruit of choice

Instructions

1. Place the dehydrated fruits in the freeze and freeze for at least 12 hours.

2. Once freezed, transfer the fruit into a high speed blender and process into a fine powder.

3. Use as desired and enjoy.

Dehydrating Fuyu Persimmon

Preparation Time: 15 minutes

Dehydration Time: 8-12 hours

Ingredients

fuyu persimmon

Instructions

1. Thoroughly wash the fuyu persimmon, dry then remove the skin.

2. Halve the fuyu persimmon and pit then cut into 1/4" thin strips.

3. Arrange the slices fuyu persimmon layers on a dehydrator tray.

4. Dehydrate for 8-12 hours at 135°F.

5. Store in a cool and dry place until ready to use.

Lime Juiced Banana Chips

Preparation Time: 15 minutes

Dehydration Time: 10-12 hours

Ingredients

1/2 cup juiced lime

15 bananas

Instructions

1. Peel the bananas then chop into 1/4" even pieces then transfer into a mixing bowl.

2. Pour the lime juice over the banana chunks into the bowl and gently stir together until well coated.

3. Leave the lime coated bananas to sit for 10 minutes then transfer and arrange on a dehydrator tray.

4. Dehydrate for 10-12 hours at 135°F until chewy, crispy and crunchy.

5. Store in a cool and dry place until ready to use.

Dehydrating Mangoes

Preparation Time: 15 minutes

Dehydration Time: 8-12 hours

Ingredients

mangoes

Instructions

1. Wash and rinse the mangoes then halve and cut the halves into thirds.

2. Using a kitchen knife gently filet the flesh from the skin and slice into 1/4" thin strips.

3. Arrange the mango strips on the dehydrator tray then dehydrate for 8-12 hours at 135°F.

4. Store in a cool and dry place until ready to use.

Simple Strawberries Dehydration

Preparation Time: 20 minutes

Dehydration Time: 6-10 hours

Ingredients

1 pound rinsed strawberries

Instructions

1. Dry the rinsed berries then hull them and chopped into 1/8" thickness.

2. Arrange the chopped berries on a dehydrator tray then dehydrate for 6-10 hours at 135°F.

3. Store in an airtight container until ready to use.

Dehydrated Banana & Nutella Leather

Preparation Time: 5 minutes

Dehydration Time: 4 hours

Ingredients

1/4 cup Nutella

4 soften small bananas

Instructions

1. Using a high speed blender, process the Nutella and bananas together until smooth and combined then spread on a dehydrator tray.

2. Dehydrate the mixture for 4 hours at 125°F until the leather is no longer sticky to touch.

3. Cut the dehydrated leather into strips then roll up together, cut into desired shapes serve and enjoy.

Dehydrated Banana & Peanut Butter Leather Roll

Preparation Time: 5 minutes

Dehydration Time: 4 hours

Ingredients

2 peeled & chopped bananas

2 tablespoons peanut butter

Instructions

1. Using a high speed blender, process the bananas and butter together until smooth and combined.

2. Transfer the mixture onto a dehydrator sheet and spread out into an even layer.

3. Dehydrate for 4-5 hours at 130°F then cut into desired sizes, roll up, serve and enjoy or store for later use.

Homemade Dehydrated Apple Chips

Preparation Time: 10 minutes

Dehydration Time: 10 hours

Ingredients

apples

juiced lime

cinnamon sugar

Instructions

1. Peel & core the apples then chop into 1/4" slices then soak with the juiced lime.

2. Arrange the chopped apples on a dehydrator tray then top with cinnamon sugar and dehydrate for 10 hours at 135°F.

3. Once leathery, remove the rings from the dehydrator, serve and enjoy or store for when ready to devour.

Dehydrating Cranberries

Preparation Time: 25 minutes

Dehydration Time: 8-12 hours

Ingredients

cranberries

water

cinnamon sugar

Instructions

1. Fill a medium sized pot with water and bring to a boil over medium high heat.

2. Add the cranberries into the and sugar into the boiling water and allow to boil for two minutes then scoop out of the hot water.

3. Arrange the popped cranberries on a dehydrating tray then dehydrate for 8-12 hours at 135°F.

4. Store in a cool dry place for later use.

Dehydrating Cherries

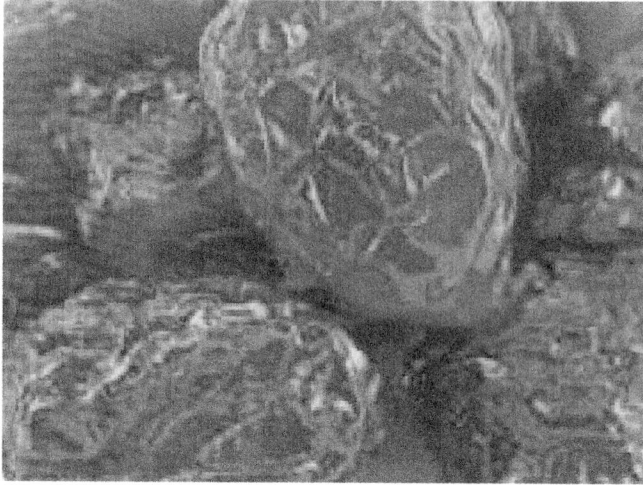

Preparation Time: 20 minutes

Dehydration Time: 12-24 hours

Ingredients

a handful of cherries

Instructions

1. Wash the cherries and dry out then remove the stems, transfer into a pitter and pit.

2. Chop the pitted cherries into desired sizes then arrange cut side up on the dehydrator tray.

3. Dehydrate the cherries for 12-24 hours for 130°F.

4. Once done, store with an airtight container in a cool and dry place for later use.

Choco Banana Leather

Preparation Time: 5 minutes

Dehydration Time: 10 hour

Ingredients

1 tablespoon brown sugar

2 tablespoons powdered cocoa

4 large bananas

Instructions

1. Using a high speed blender, add in the bananas, cocoa, sugar and process until combined and smooth.

2. Transfer the mixture onto a dehydrator tray and roll out into 1/4" thickness.

3. Dehydrate for 10 hours at 130°F flipping the leather half way through the Dehydration Time.

4. Store in a cool and dry place until ready to use.

Dehydrating Blanched Strawberries

Preparation Time: 20 minutes

Dehydration Time: 6-12 hours

Ingredients

1 cup sugar

1 cup white corn syrup

2 cups water

2 quarts fresh strawberries

Instructions

1. Using a medium sized saucepan, pour in the corn syrup, sugar, cups of water and bring to a boil.

2. Slice the strawberries into bits then add into the boiling syrup mix and blanch, simmering for 10 minutes.

3. Take the pan off the heat and allow to sit for 30 minutes then drain the fruit of the syrup.

4. Arrange the strawberry slices on the dehydrator tray and dehydrate for 6-12 hours at 130°F.

5. Place the dried berries in an airtight container and store in a cool and dry place.

Dehydrating Bananas

Preparation Time: 10 minutes

Dehydration Time: 8-12 hours

Ingredients

bananas

Instructions

1. Peel the bananas then chop into 1/4" thick chunks and arrange on a dehydrator tray.

2. Dehydrate the bananas for 8-12 hours at 135°F until very dry.

3. Store in a cool and dry place until ready to use.

Dehydrating Blueberries

Preparation Time: 10 minutes

Dehydration Time: 8-10

Ingredients

a handful of blueberries

Instructions

1. Thoroughly wash the blueberries then dry, stem and arrange on the dehydrator tray.

2. Dehydrate the berries for 8-10 hours at 115°F until dry.

3. Store in a cool and dry place until ready to use.

Buttery Banana Chips

Preparation Time: 10 minutes

Dehydration Time: 8 hours

Ingredients

1/4 cup peanut butter

5 large bananas

Instructions

1. Chop the bananas into 1/4" thick slices then coat the chops with the peanut butter until well covered.

2. Arrange the coated bananas on a dehydrator tray then dehydrate for 8 hours at 160°C.

3. Store in an airtight container until later.

Dehydrated Lime Drizzled Berries

Preparation Time: 8 minutes

Dehydration Time: 15-18 hours

Ingredients

1 lime juice

a bunch of raspberries

Instructions

1. Thoroughly wash and dry the raspberries then arrange on a dehydrator tray.

2. Drizzle the dried raspberries with the lime juice.

3. Dehydrate for 15-18 hours at 135°F.

4. Store in an airtight container until ready to use.

Dehydrating Plums

Preparation Time: 15 minutes

Dehydration Time: 4-6 hours

Ingredients

Italian plums

Instructions

1. Wash the plums and dry then horizontally half and pit.

2. Twist each half then remove and dispose the pit.

3. Arrange the plum halves cut side down on a dehydrator tray then place in a dehydrator.

4. Dehydrate at 145°F for 4-6 hours, flipping over halfway through Dehydration Time.

5. Once dry, store in a cool & dry place.

Dehydrating Pineapple

Preparation Time: 15 minutes

Dehydration Time: 12-16 hours

Ingredients

pineapples

Instructions

1. Rinse & scrub the pineapples using clean water then chop into 1/2" chunks.

2. Arrange the chopped pineapples on a dehydrator tray then dehydrate for 12-16 hours at 135°F flipping the pineapples halfway through Dehydration Time.

3. Using an airtight container, store and keep in a cool & dry place.

Dehydrated Honey Glazed Mangoes

Preparation Time: 10 minutes

Dehydration Time: 10-12 hours

Ingredients

1/4 cup juiced lime

1 tablespoon raw honey

5 ripe mangoes

Instructions

1. Using a small mixing bowl, add in the juiced lime, honey and combine together until the honey is dissolved.

2. Peel the mangoes then cut into small even slices then coat with the honey and lime mixture.

3. Arrange the coated mango slices on the dehydrator sheet then dehydrate at 135°F for 10-12 hours.

4. Store in a cool and dry place until ready to use.

Coconut Chunks

Preparation Time: 13 minutes

Dehydration Time: 8-10 hours

Ingredients:

coconut

Instructions

1. Cut the coconut flesh into 1/4" slices then arrange on a dehydrator tray.

2. Dehydrate the coconut chunks until dry at 130°F for 8-10 hours.

3. Store in a cool and dry place until ready to use.

Dehydrating Grapes

Preparation Time: 10 minutes

Dehydration Time: 24-48 hours

Ingredients

seedless red grapes

Instructions

1. Thoroughly wash the grapes then dry, halve and arrange on the dehydrator tray.

2. Dehydrate for 24-48 hours at 135°F until dry.

3. Store in a cool and dry place until ready to use.

Dehydrating Peaches

Preparation Time: 15 minutes

Dehydration Time: 8-12 hours

Ingredients

peaches

Instructions

1. Thoroughly wash the peaches, dry then remove the skin.

2. Halve the peaches and pit then cut into 1/4" thin strips.

3. Arrange the slices peach layers on a dehydrator tray.

4. Dehydrate for 8-12 hours at 135°F.

5. Store in a cool and dry place until ready to use.

Dehydrated Marshmallows

Preparation Time: 0 minute

Dehydration Time: 3 hours

Ingredients

1 bag of marshmallows

Instructions

1. Arrange the marshmallows on a dehydrator tray.

2. Dehydrate for 3 hours at 135°F.

4. Store in a cool and dry place until ready to use.

Simple Milk Yogurt

Preparation Time: 20 minutes

Dehydration Time: 8-12 hours

Ingredients

1/2-gallon milk

2 tablespoons plain yogurt

Instructions

1. Using a large pot placed over medium heat, heat the milk up until it starts to bubble but not boil.

2. Take the milk off the heat and allow to cool down to 110°F meanwhile use the dehydrator to preheat 2 large jars up to 110°F.

3. Add the tablespoons of yogurt into the cooled milk, stir together then divided into the preheated jars from the dehydrator and cover.

4. Return the dehydrating jars into the dehydrator and dehydrate for 8-12 hours at 105°F-110°F.

5. Refrigerate until chilled as desired then serve and enjoy or store for use later.

JERKY RECIPES

Chicken Breast Jerky

Preparation Time: 20 minutes

Dehydration Time: 12-24 hours

Ingredients

1/2 cup apple cider vinegar

1 cup vegetable oil

1 teaspoon black pepper

1 tablespoon onion salt

1 tablespoon powdered garlic

3 tablespoons soy sauce

4 chopped chicken breast

Instructions

1. Using a large mixing bowl, add in all the ingredients (except the chicken) and combine together.

2. Add in the chicken pieces and stir in until properly coated with the marinade then allow to marinate for 12 hours or more.

3. Once marinated, transfer the chicken pieces onto a dehydrator sheet and dehydrate for 12-24 hours at 145°F over medium high heat.

4. Once dehydrated, check for dryness and ensure that all the moisture is out then store in an airtight container for up to 4 months.

London Broil Jerky

Preparation Time: 10 minutes

Dehydration Time: 8 hours

Ingredients

1 teaspoon paprika

1 teaspoon black pepper

1 teaspoon ground ginger

1 teaspoon powdered onion

1 cup apple cider vinegar

1 teaspoon powdered chili

1 teaspoon powdered garlic

2 ounces juiced lime

2 cups juiced pineapple

2 tablespoons smoked salt

3 pounds sliced thin broil London

6 ounces coconut aminos

Instructions

1. Add all the ingredients into a large mixing bowl and combine together until mixed.

2. Place the London broil slices in the spice mix and allow to marinate for at least 24 hours.

3. Transfer the dehydrated meat slices onto a dehydrator sheet then place inside the dehydrator.

4. Dehydrate for 8 hours at 150°F then store and use when needed.

Venison Roast Jerky

Preparation Time: 15 minutes

Dehydration Time: 4 hours

Ingredients

1/4 teaspoon powdered onion

1/4 teaspoon powdered garlic

1/4 teaspoon red pepper flakes

1 tablespoon honey

1 pound sliced thin venison roast

4 tablespoons coconut aminos

4 tablespoons Worcestershire sauce

salt & black pepper, to taste

Instructions

1. Completely skin the venison roast then freeze for an hour and thin slice into 1/4" thickness and 1" wide.

2. Using a stainless steel, add in the Worcestershire sauce, coconut aminos, salt, black pepper, onion & garlic powder, honey, pepper flakes and combine together.

3. Add the roast slices into the sauce mix then cover, refrigerate and allow to marinade for 24 hour or more.

4. Once marinated, drain the roast of the sauce mix and transfer onto dehydrator sheets and place in a dehydrator.

5. Dehydrate for 4 hours at 160°F until the jerky is finished.

6. Transfer into air tight containers and store for months, using when needed.

Lean Beef Beer Jerky

Preparation Time: 15 minutes

Dehydration Time: 6 hours

Ingredients

1/2 cup light soy sauce

1 tablespoon honey

1 tablespoon liquid smoke

2 minced garlic cloves

700g lean cut beef

black pepper, to taste

a can of Guinness draught

Instructions

1. Cut off all the excess fat from the beef then freeze for 2 hours and slice into 1/4" thick slices.

2. Using a large mixing bowl, add in the remaining spice ingredient and combine together.

3. Place the beef slices into the spice mix and toss around then cover and leave to marinade for 8 hours.

4. Once marinated, drain the beef slice of the marinade mix then arrange on a dehydrator sheet.

5. Transfer the dehydrator sheet into a dehydrator and dehydrate for an hour at 165°F.

6. Reduce the heat to 155°F then continue to dehydrate for 5 hours until dry.

7. Store in an airtight container until ready to use.

Smoky Beef Steak Jerky

Preparation Time: 15 minutes

Dehydration Time: 7 hours

Ingredients

1/4 cup BBQ sauce

1/2 cup smoke marinade

1 teaspoon powdered onion

2 tablespoons brown sugar

chopped round beef steak

a pinch of cayenne pepper

kosher salt & black pepper, to taste

Instructions

1. Skim the excess fat from the beef steak then combine the remaining ingredients together.

2. Add the sliced beef steak into the marinade mixture, toss and allow to refrigerate for 24 hours.

3. Drain the beef off the marinade mixture then arrange on a dehydrator sheet and dehydrate for 7 hours at 180°F.

4. Flip the beef slices halfway through the dehydration time then store in an airtight container until ready to use.

Simple Eggplant Jerky

Preparation Time: 2 hours

Dehydration Time: 10 hours

Ingredients

1 cup avocado oil

1 cup balsamic vinegar

2 large eggplants

2 teaspoons paprika

2 minced garlic cloves

sea salt & black pepper, to taste

Instructions

1. Rinse, drain and chop the eggplant into thin slices then quarter them into small sized pieces, cutting the bottom off.

2. Add the remaining ingredients into a large mixing bowl and combine together then add in the chopped eggplants and toss until well coated.

3. Set the marinade mix aside for 2 hours to allow the eggplants to marinate then arrange on a dehydrating tray.

4. Sprinkle the eggplants with extra salt & pepper if desired then dehydrate at 115°F for 15 hours.

5. Store using an airtight container in a dry place until ready to use.

Marinated Dehydrated Lamb Jerky

Preparation Time: 15 minutes

Dehydration Time: 6 hours

Ingredients

1/3 cup low salt soy sauce

1/2 teaspoon freshly ground black pepper

1 tablespoon oregano

1 teaspoon powdered garlic

1 1/2 teaspoons powdered onion

3 tablespoons Worcestershire sauce

3 pounds boneless lamb leg, fats cut off

Instructions

1. Freeze the lamb leg for an hour, meanwhile, combine the remaining ingredients together until combined.

2. Vertically slice the lamb leg into thin slices then arrange in in large baking dish.

3. Coat the lamb slices with the ingredients mixture until well covered then cover the dish and refrigerate to marinate for 12 hours.

4. Once marinated, arrange the lamb slices on the dehydrator tray and dehydrate for 6 hours 145°F.

5. Once dried & crispy, store and keep in a cool dry place.

MUSHROOM RECIPES

Simple Dehydrated Portabella Mushroom

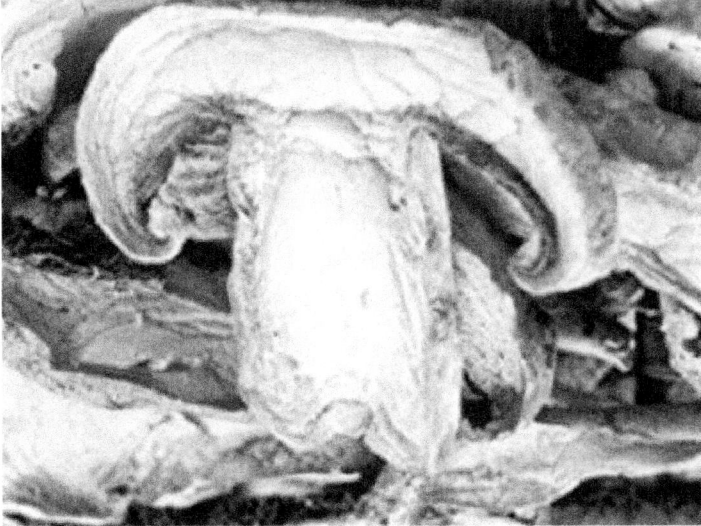

Preparation Time: 15 minutes

Dehydration Time: 6 hours

Ingredients

baby portebellos mushrooms

Instructions

1. Wash and dry the portebellos then chop into thin sizes then arrange on a dehydrator tray.

2. Place the tray inside the dehydrator and dehydrate until all the moisture is removed for 6 hours over low setting.

3. Store using an airtight container in a dry place.

Teriyaki Portabella Mushroom Jerky

Prep Time: 8 hours 15 minutes

Dehydration Time: 12 hours

Ingredients

1/4 cup low salt tamari

1/2" chopped ginger

1 teaspoon sriracha

1 minced garlic clove

1 1/2 teaspoon avocado oil

2 tablespoons brown sugar

2 large portabella mushroom caps

3 tablespoons rice vinegar

Instructions

1. Rinse & dry the mushroom caps then chop into 1/2" thick pieces and set aside.

2. Using a large mixing bowl, combine all the ingredients together until mixed.

3. Add the mushroom pieces into the marinade mixture, toss until coated then set aside to marinate for 8 hours.

4. Drain the mushrooms of the marinade then arrange on a dehydrator tray and place in a dehydrator.

5. Dehydrate for 12 hours at 125°F until all the moisture are out.

6. Store using an air tight container in a cool and dry place until ready to use.

Crispy Mushroom Caps

Preparation Time: 15 minutes

Dehydration Time: 5 hours

Ingredients

1/2 teaspoon dried parsley

1/2 teaspoon sea salt & powdered garlic

1 pound mushrooms caps

1 tablespoon juiced lime

Instructions

1. Cut the ends of the mushroom off then chop into 1/2" thick slices and set aside.

2. Add the remaining ingredients into a mixing bowl then place in the mushroom pieces and incorporate with the marinade mixture.

3. Allow the mushrooms to marinate then drain and spread on a dehydrator tray and transfer into a dehydrator.

4. Dehydrate on high until crispy for 5 hours.

5. Serve and enjoy immediately or store in an air tight container until ready to use.

Porcini Bouillon Sauce Bombs

Preparation Time: 25 minutes

Dehydration Time: 10 hours

Ingredients

1 teaspoon fish sauce

2 tablespoons water

2 tablespoons soy sauce

2 teaspoon powdered gelatin

2 ounces dried porcini mushrooms

2 1/2 teaspoon sea salt

2 1/2 tablespoons powdered onion

Instructions

1. Grind and crush the porcini mushrooms into a fine powder then add in the salt, gelatin, onion powder and combine together.

2. Add the soy & fish sauce into the mushroom powder ingredients and incorporate together.

3. Pour in the tablespoons of water combine until mixed then knead for a few seconds.

4. Roll the dough out into 1/2" thickness then cut out into 1/2" cubes and arrange on a dehydrator tray.

5. Place the tray in the dehydrator and dehydrate at 125°F for 10 hours.

6. Once done, store in an air tight container until ready to use.

Dehydrating Mushrooms

Preparation Time: 10 minutes

Dehydration Time: 4-6 hours

Ingredients

portobello mushrooms

Instructions

1. Thoroughly wash and dry the mushrooms then chop into desired sizes.

2. Arrange the chopped mushrooms on a dehydrator tray then dehydrate for 4-6 hours at 125°F.

3. Once dehydrated, store in an airtight container until ready to use.

END

Thank you for reading my book.

Michelle Vazquez

Printed in Great Britain
by Amazon